Alfred's Basic Piano Library

Piano

Notespeller Book
Level 1A

Gayle Kowalchyk • E. L. Lancaster

Second Edition
Copyright © MCMXCV by Alfred Publishing Co.. Inc.
All rights reserved.   Printed in USA.

Cover illustration and interior art by Russ Cohen

Instructions for Use

1. This NOTESPELLER is designed to be used with Alfred's Basic Piano Library, LESSON BOOK 1A. It can also serve as an effective supplement for other piano methods.

2. This book is coordinated page-by-page with the LESSON BOOK, and assignments are ideally made according to the instructions in the upper right corner of each page of the NOTESPELLER.

3. This NOTESPELLER reinforces note reading concepts presented in the LESSON BOOK through written exercises. Note and interval identification exercises are presented throughout the book to provide the necessary systematic reinforcement for the student.

Gayle Kowalchyk
E. L. Lancaster

Contents

White Keys

Piano keys are named for the first seven letters of the alphabet.

A   B   C   D   E   F   G

1. Write the missing letter names from the music alphabet on each line.

- **A**   ___   **C**   ___   **E**   ___   **G**
- ___   **B**   ___   ___   **E**   **F**   ___
- **A**   ___   ___   **D**   ___   ___   ___

2. Write the name of every white key on the keyboard, beginning with the given A.

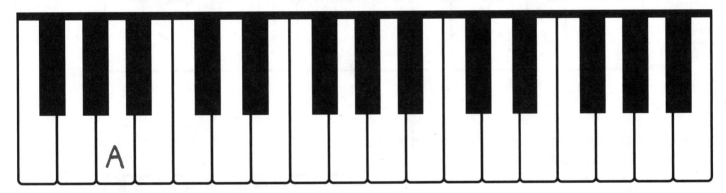

3. Write the letter name on each key marked X.

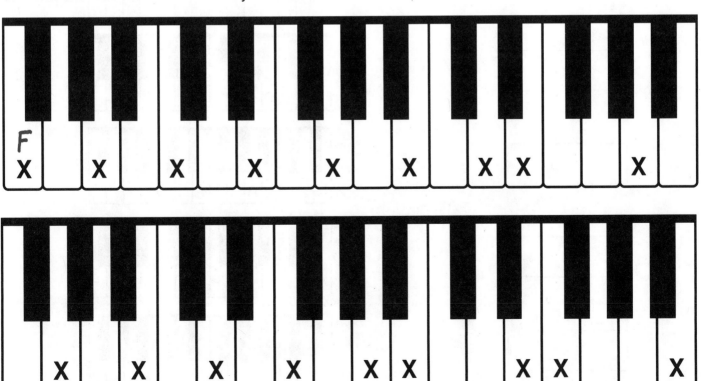

4

Use with page 22.

Middle C Position

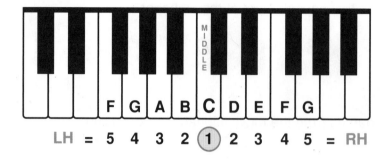

1. Write the names of the keys in the MIDDLE C POSITION on the keyboard.

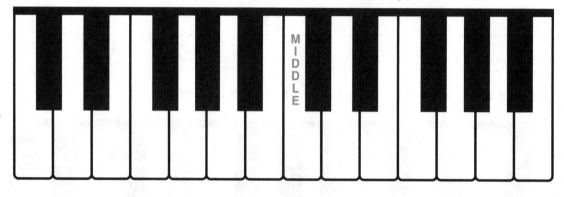

2. Draw lines connecting the dots to match the left hand finger number with the key that it plays in MIDDLE C POSITION.

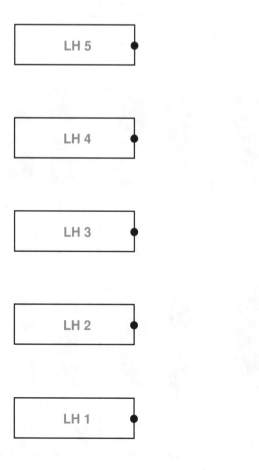

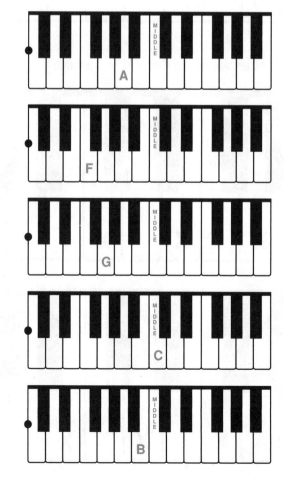

Middle C Position

1. Write the letter name from the MIDDLE C POSITION on each key marked X.

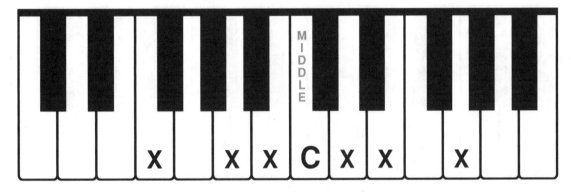

2. Draw lines connecting the dots to match the right hand finger number with the key that it plays in MIDDLE C POSITION.

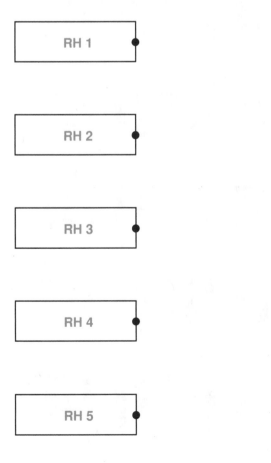

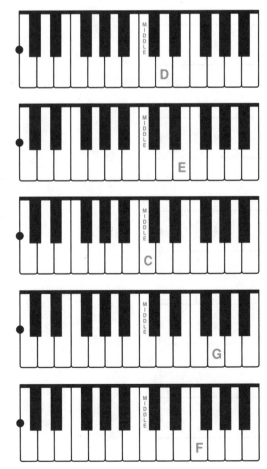

Use with page 23.

C Position

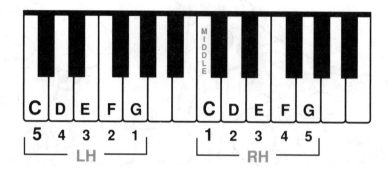

1. Write the names of the keys in the C POSITION on the keyboard.

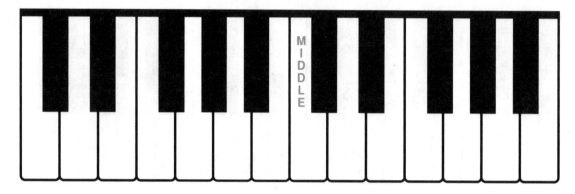

2. Draw lines connecting the dots to match the left hand finger number with the key that it plays in C POSITION.

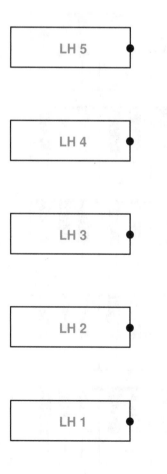

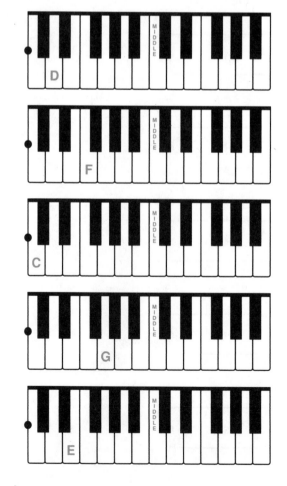

C Position

1. Write the letter name from the C POSITION on each key marked X.

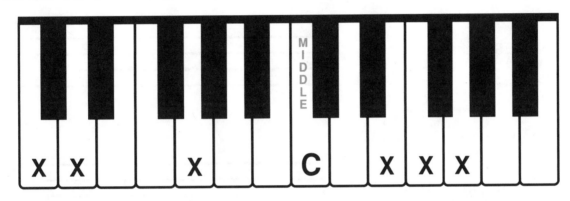

2. Draw lines connecting the dots to match the right hand finger number with the key that it plays in C POSITION.

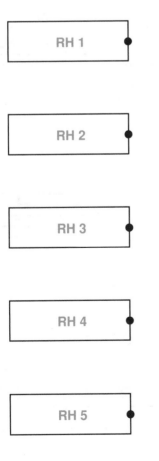

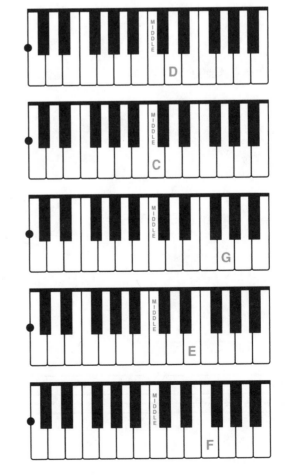

RH 1

RH 2

RH 3

RH 4

RH 5

Use with page 27.

The Staff

Music is written on a STAFF of 5 lines and 4 spaces.

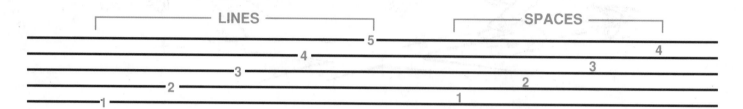

1. Number the LINES on the staff.

2. Number the SPACES on the staff.

Some notes are written on LINES.

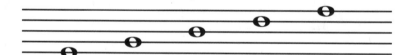

Some notes are written in SPACES.

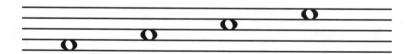

3. Circle each LINE NOTE.   4. Circle each SPACE NOTE.

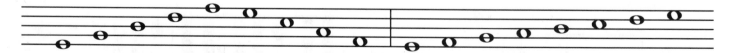

The Bass Clef

The BASS CLEF SIGN 𝄢 locates the F below the middle of the keyboard.

This is the F line.

The F line passes between the two dots of the F clef sign!

The BASS CLEF SIGN came from the letter F:

1. Draw five BASS CLEF SIGNS.

2. Circle each F in the bass clef.

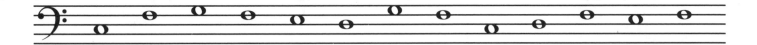

The Bass Clef

By moving up or down from the F line, you can name any note on the bass staff.

1. Write the notes in the BASS staff under the squares. Use WHOLE NOTES.

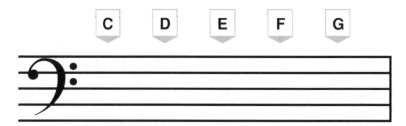

2. Write the name of each note in the square below it—then play and say the note names.

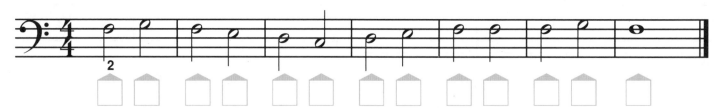

3. Write the name of each note in the square below it. The letters in each group of squares will spell a familiar word. Play and say the note names.

The Treble Clef

The TREBLE CLEF SIGN locates the G above the middle of the keyboard.

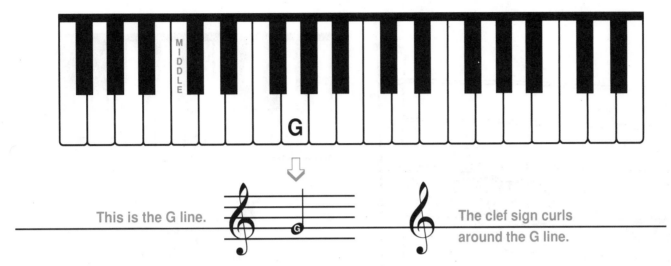

This is the G line.

The clef sign curls around the G line.

The TREBLE CLEF SIGN came from the letter G:

1. Draw five TREBLE CLEF SIGNS.

2. Circle each G in the treble clef.

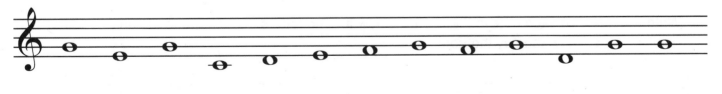

Use with page 31.

The Treble Clef

By moving up or down from the G line, you can name any note on the treble staff.

1. Write the notes in the TREBLE staff under the squares. Use WHOLE NOTES.

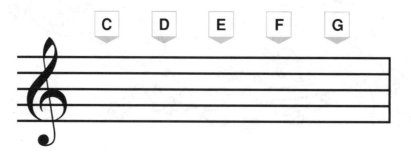

2. Write the name of each note in the square below it—then play and say the note names.

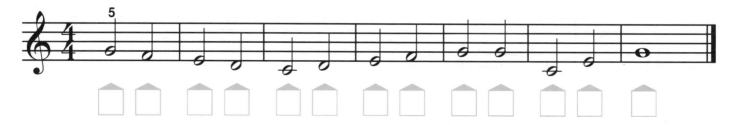

3. Write the name of each note in the square below it. The letters in each group of squares will spell a familiar word. Play and say the note names.

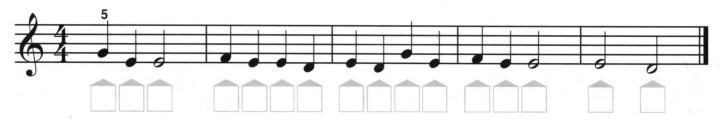

Use with page 32.

The Grand Staff

The TREBLE STAFF and the BASS STAFF are joined together with a BRACE and a BAR LINE to make a GRAND STAFF.

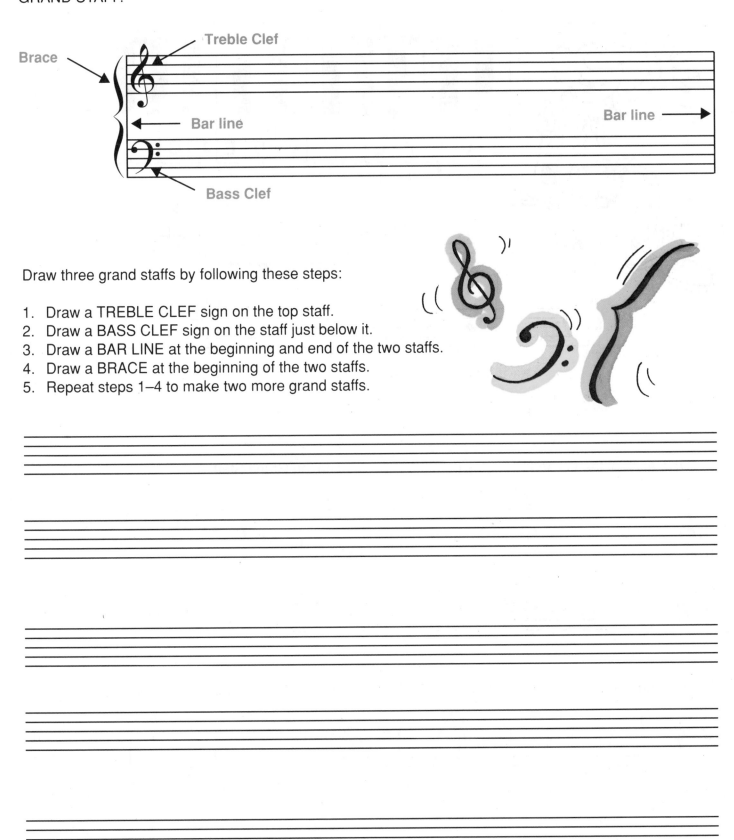

Draw three grand staffs by following these steps:

1. Draw a TREBLE CLEF sign on the top staff.
2. Draw a BASS CLEF sign on the staff just below it.
3. Draw a BAR LINE at the beginning and end of the two staffs.
4. Draw a BRACE at the beginning of the two staffs.
5. Repeat steps 1–4 to make two more grand staffs.

Use with page 33.

C Position on the Grand Staff

1. Circle each of the LH and RH notes from the C position on the Grand Staff.

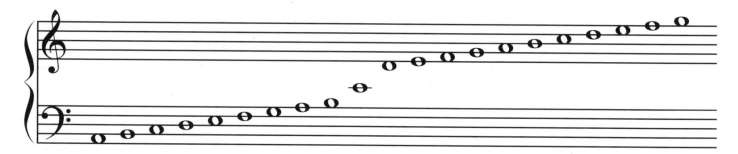

2. Write the name of each note in the square below it—then play and say the note names.

C Position

1. Print the letter names for both the left hand and right hand C POSITION on the keyboard.

2. Draw a line to connect each note on the staff to the appropriate key on the keyboard.

3. Draw lines connecting the dots on the matching boxes.

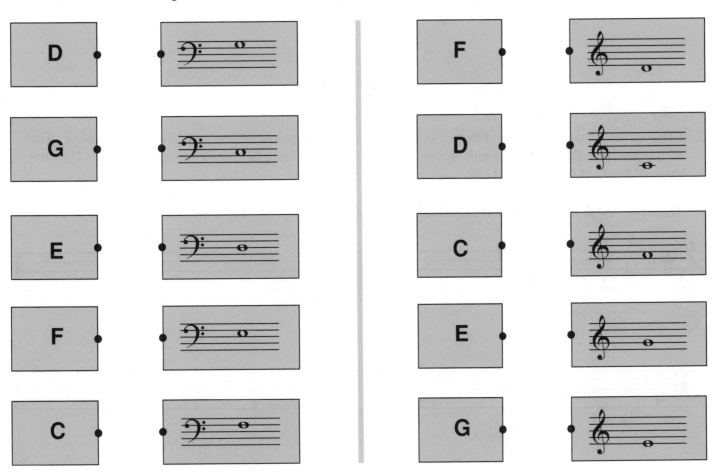

Use with page 36.

2nds

The distance from any white key to the next white key, up or down, is called a **2nd**.

2nds are written LINE-SPACE or SPACE-LINE.

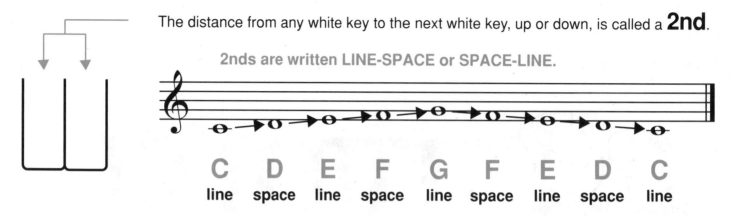

C	D	E	F	G	F	E	D	C
line	space	line	space	line	space	line	space	line

1. Draw a half note UP a 2nd from the given note in the first four measures of each line below. Turn all the stems in the treble clef UP. Turn all the stems in the bass clef DOWN.

2. Write the name of each note in the square below it—then play and say the note names.

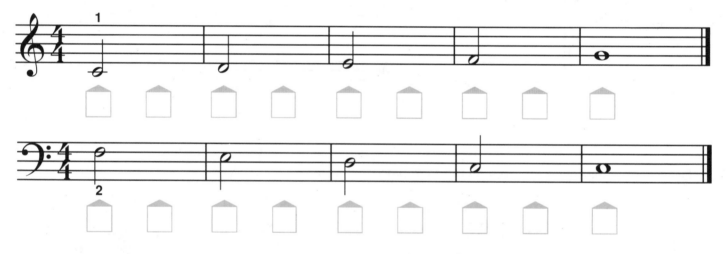

3. Draw a half note DOWN a 2nd from the given note in the first four measures of each line below. Turn all the stems in the treble clef UP. Turn the stems of D, E, F and G in the bass clef DOWN. Turn the stem of the C in the bass clef UP.

4. Write the name of each note in the square below it—then play and say the note names.

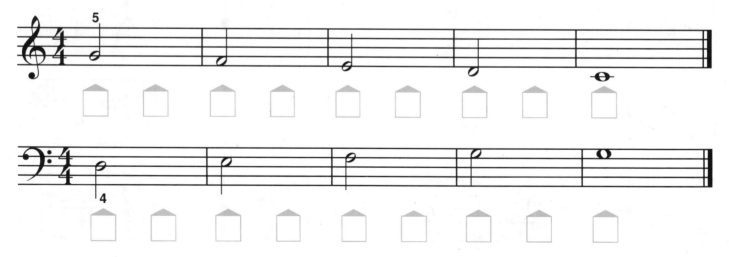

3rds

When you skip a white key, the interval is a **3rd**.

3rds are written LINE-LINE or SPACE-SPACE.

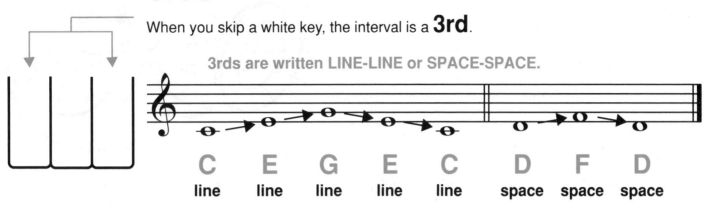

C   E   G   E   C   D   F   D

line   line   line   line   line   space   space   space

1. Draw a half note UP a 3rd from the given note in the first four measures of each line below. Turn all the stems in the treble clef UP. Turn all the stems in the bass clef DOWN.

2. Write the name of each note in the square below it—then play and say the note names.

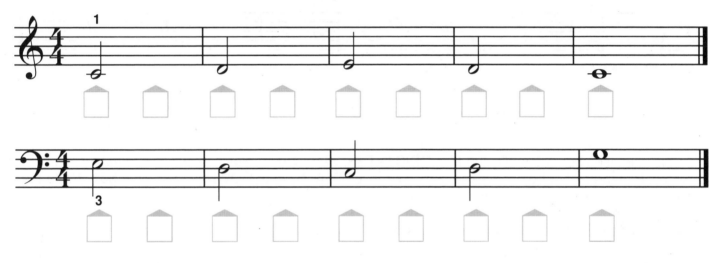

3. Draw a half note DOWN a 3rd from the given note in the first four measures of each line below. Turn all the stems in the treble clef UP. Turn the stems of D, E, F and G in the bass clef DOWN. Turn the stem of the C in the bass clef UP.

4. Write the name of each note in the square below it—then play and say the note names.

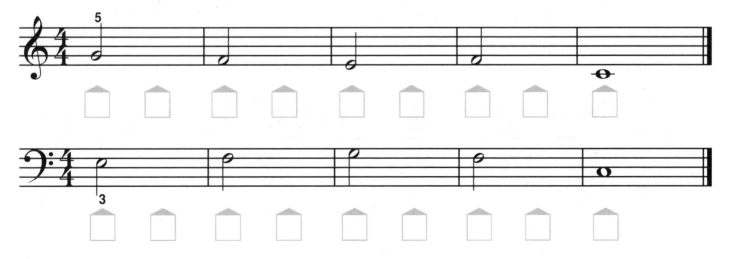

Use with page 40.

Melodic Intervals

Notes played SEPARATELY make a MELODY.

Intervals between these notes are MELODIC INTERVALS.

1. Write the names of the MELODIC INTERVALS (2nd or 3rd) in the boxes.

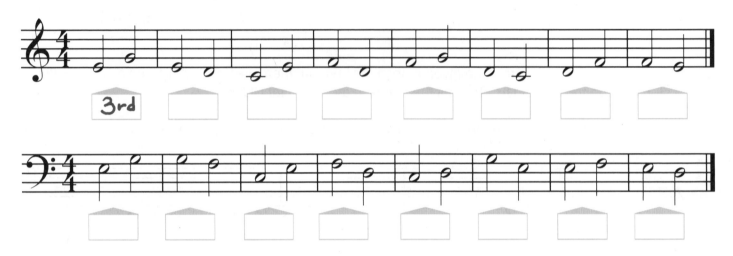

3rd

2. In the exercises below, identify the MELODIC INTERVALS in the C Position. If the interval moves UP, write UP in the higher box above the staff; if it moves DOWN, write DOWN in the higher box. Write the name of the interval (2nd or 3rd) in the lower box.

3. Write the names of the notes in the squares below the staff.

Down
2nd

4. Play and say the note names.

Harmonic Intervals

Notes played TOGETHER make HARMONY.

Intervals between these notes are HARMONIC INTERVALS.

1. Write the names of the HARMONIC INTERVALS (2nd or 3rd) in the boxes.

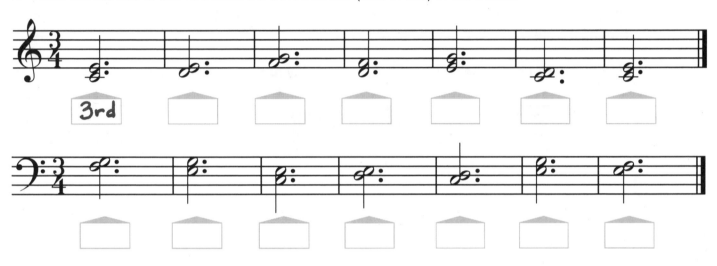

3rd

2. In the exercises below, write the names of the notes in the squares above the staff. Write the name of the lower note in the lower square; the name of the higher note in the higher square.

3. Write the names of the HARMONIC INTERVALS (2nd or 3rd) in the boxes below the staff.

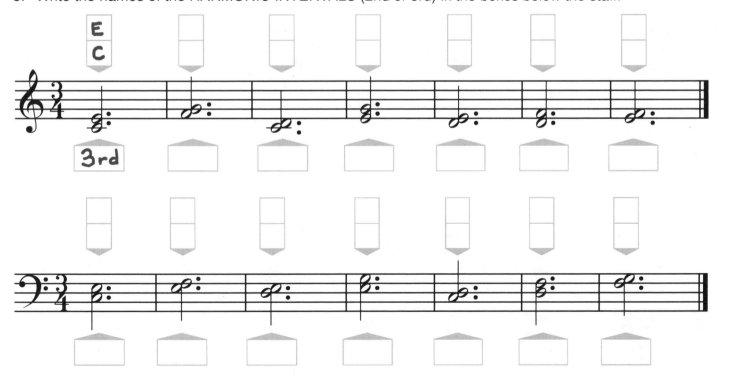

E
C

3rd

Use with page 44.

4ths

When you skip 2 white keys, the interval is a **4th**.

4ths are written LINE-SPACE or SPACE-LINE.

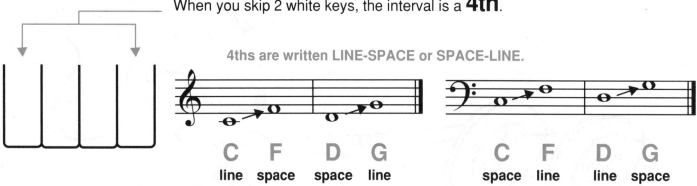

1. Draw a half note UP a 4th from the given note in each measure below. Turn all the stems in the treble clef UP. Turn all the stems in the bass clef DOWN.

2. Write the name of each note in the square below it—then play and say the note names.

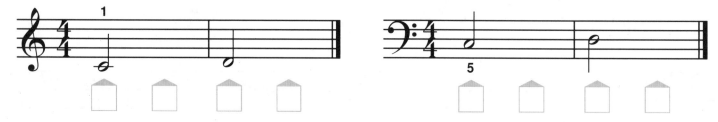

3. Draw a half note DOWN a 4th from the given note in each measure below. Turn all the stems in the treble clef UP. Turn the stems of D, E, F and G in the bass clef DOWN. Turn the stem of the C in the bass clef UP.

4. Write the name of each note in the square below it—then play and say the note names.

5. Circle each HARMONIC 4th.

Note and Interval Review

1. Write the name of each note in the square below it—then play and say the note names.

2. Write the notes from the C POSITION in the TREBLE STAFF under the squares. Use WHOLE NOTES.

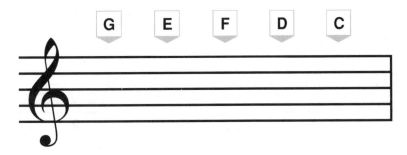

3. Write the notes from the C POSITION in the BASS STAFF under the squares. Use WHOLE NOTES.

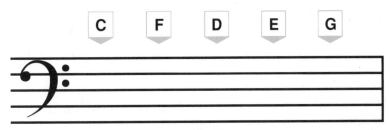

4. Draw a half note UP from the given note in each measure below to make the indicated melodic interval. Turn all the stems in the treble clef UP. Turn all the stems in the bass clef DOWN.

5. Write the name of each note in the square below it.

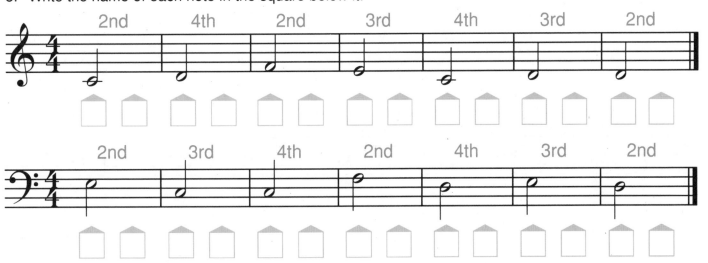

Use with page 48.

5ths

When you skip 3 white keys, the interval is a **5th**.

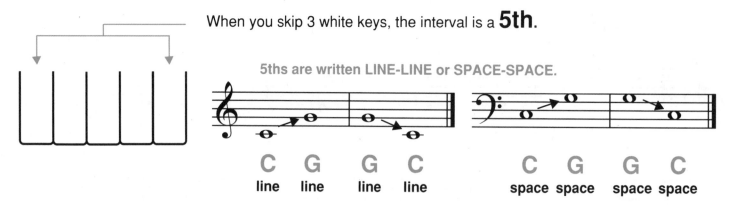

1. Draw a half note UP a 5th from each C and DOWN a 5th from each G on each staff below. Turn all the stems in the treble clef UP. Turn the stem of the G in the bass clef DOWN. Turn the stem of the C in the bass clef UP.

2. Write the name of each note in the square below it—then play and say the note name.

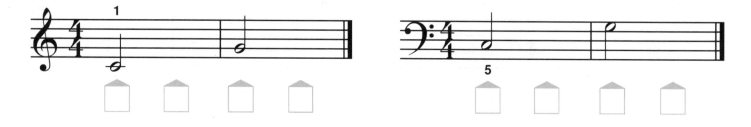

3. Draw a whole note ABOVE the given note in each measure below to make the indicated harmonic interval.

4. Write the names of the notes in the squares. Write the name of the lower note in the lower square; the name of the higher note in the higher square.

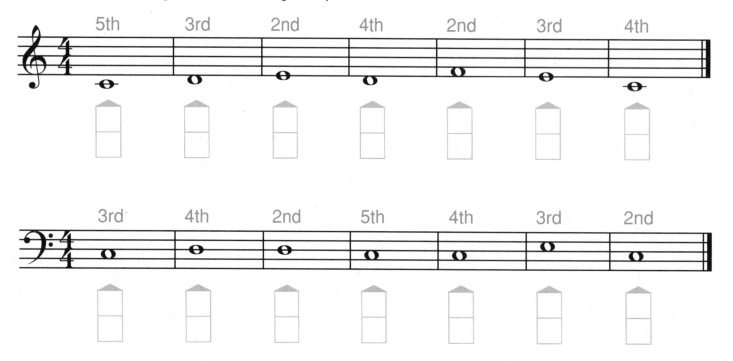

G Position on the Grand Staff

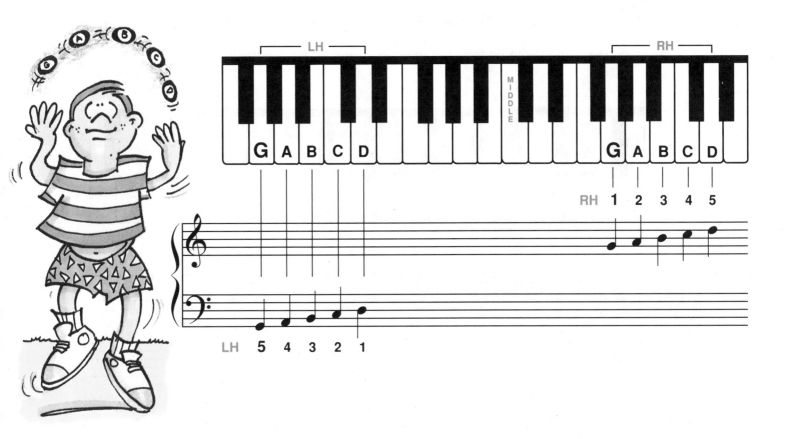

1. Circle each of the LH and RH notes from the G position on the grand staff.

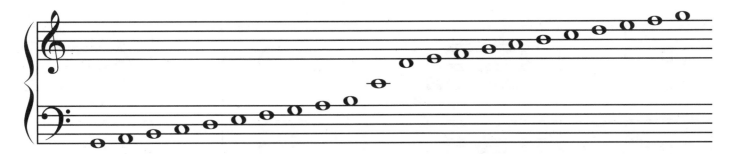

2. Write the name of each note in the square below it—then play and say the note names.

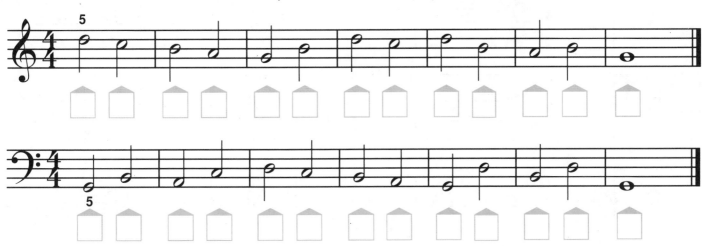

Use with page 51.

G Position

1. Print the letter names for both the left hand and right hand G POSITION on the keyboard.

2. Draw a line to connect each note on the staff to the appropriate key on the keyboard.

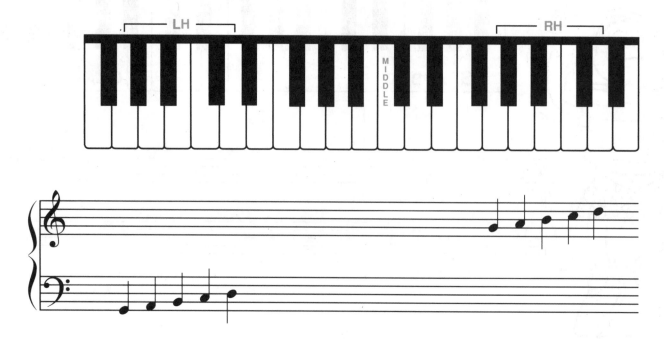

3. Draw lines connecting the dots on the matching boxes.

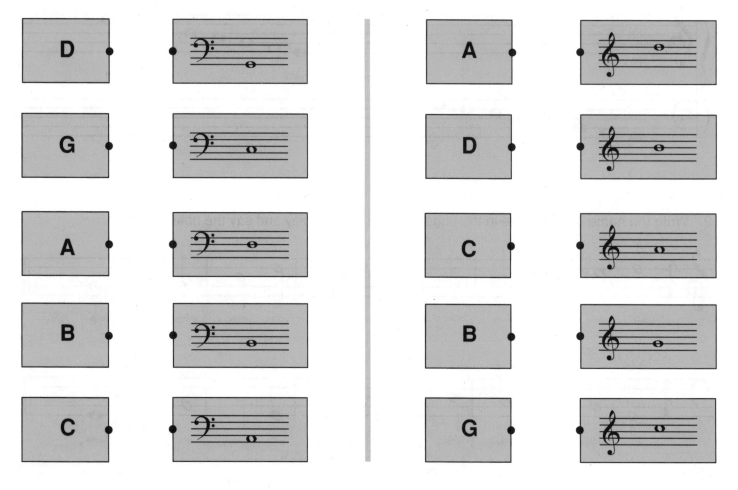

Note Review

Solve the cross-word puzzle by writing the names of the notes in the squares.

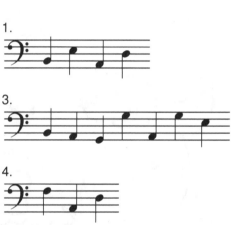

Across

Down

Use with page 54.

Note and Interval Review

1. Write the notes from the G POSITION in the TREBLE STAFF under the squares. Use WHOLE NOTES.

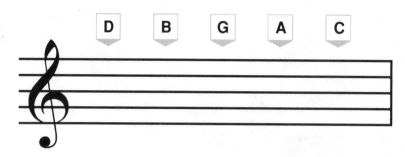

2. Write the notes from the G POSITION in the BASS STAFF under the squares. Use WHOLE NOTES.

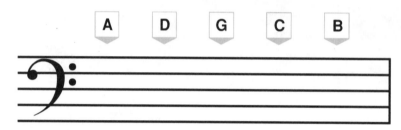

3. Draw a whole note BELOW the given note to make the indicated harmonic interval.

4. Write the names of the notes in the squares below the staff. Write the name of the lower note in the lower square; the name of the higher note in the higher square.

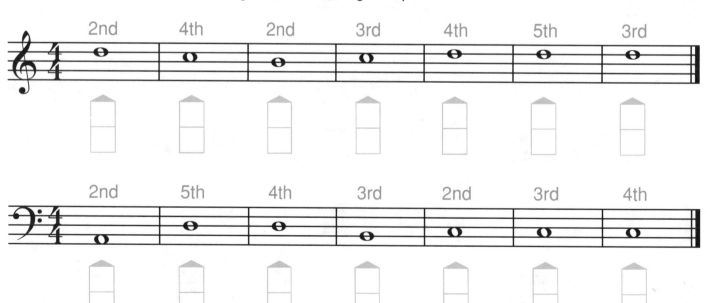

Sharp

1. Draw a SHARP (♯) before each C on the staffs below.

2. Write the name of each note in the square below it—then play and say the note names.

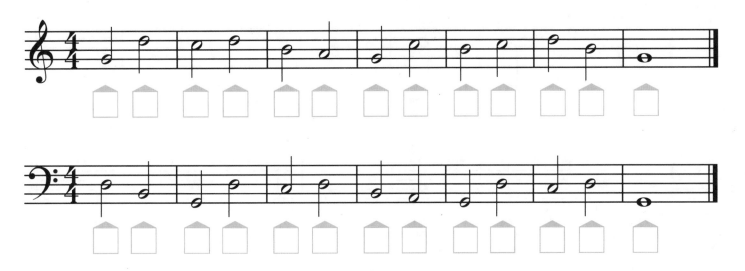

3. Draw lines connecting the dots, to match the name of the sharped note to its location on the keyboard.

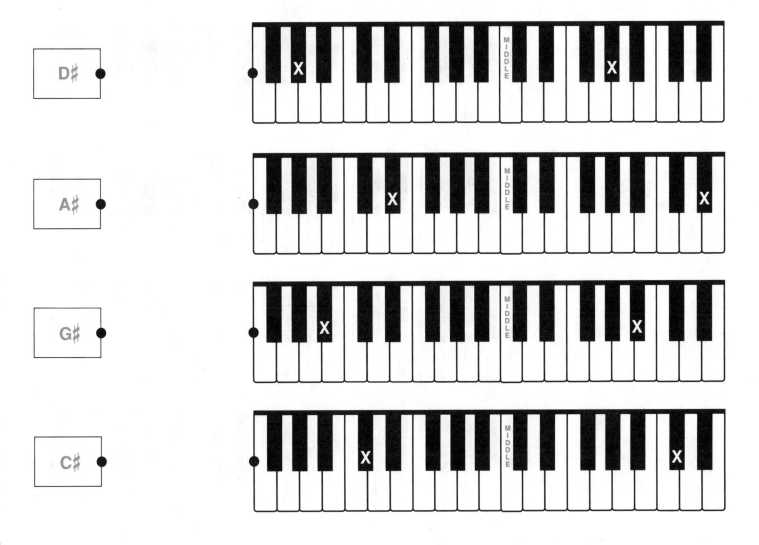

Flat

1. Draw a FLAT (♭) before each B on the staffs below.

2. Write the name of each note in the square below it—then play and say the note names.

3. Draw lines connecting the dots, to match the name of the flatted note to its location on the keyboard.

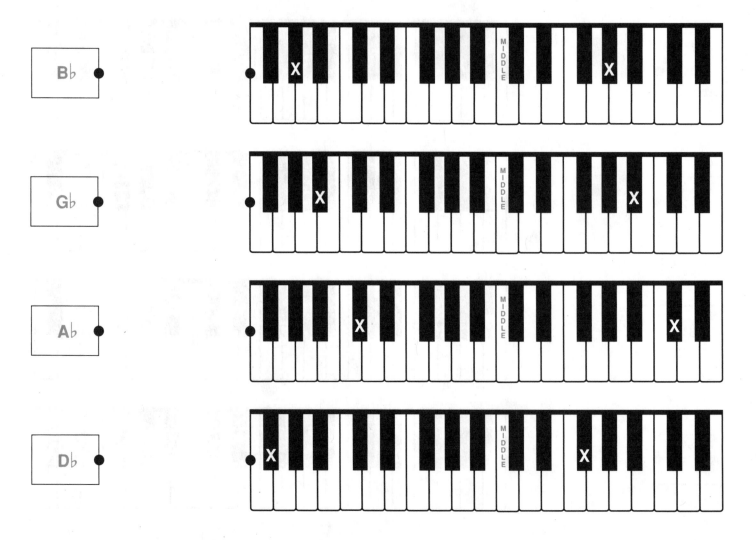

Note Review

Draw lines connecting the dots on the matching boxes.

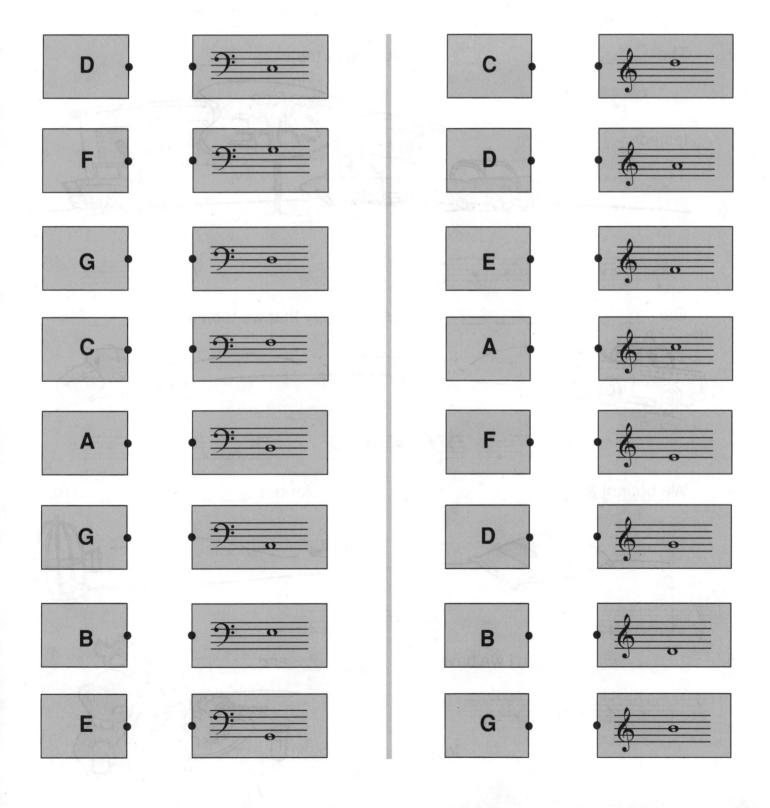

Note Review

Use with page 58.

Write the name of each note on the line below it to complete the sentences.

1. __ __ __   __ __ __ __ __ __   his mother to let him stay in __ __ __ __ .

2. The __ __ __   __ __ __   ordered at the __ __ __ __

   tasted __ __ __ .

3. Our __ __ __ __ __ __ __ __ __ __   was so heavy that we took a __ __ __ .

4. We bought a __ __ __ __   of __ __ __ __ __   for our __ __ __ __ __ __   bird.

5. __ __ __ __ !   Can't we have __ __ __ __ __   and

   __ __ __ __ __ __ __ __   for dinner again?

Interval Review

1. Draw a half note BELOW the given note to make the indicated melodic interval. Turn all the stems in the treble clef UP. Turn the stems of G, A, B and C in the bass clef UP. Turn the stem of the D in the bass clef DOWN.

2. Write the name of each note in the square below it.

3. Draw a whole note ABOVE the given note to make the indicated harmonic interval.

4. Write the names of the notes in the squares. Write the name of the lower note in the lower square; the name of the higher note in the higher square.

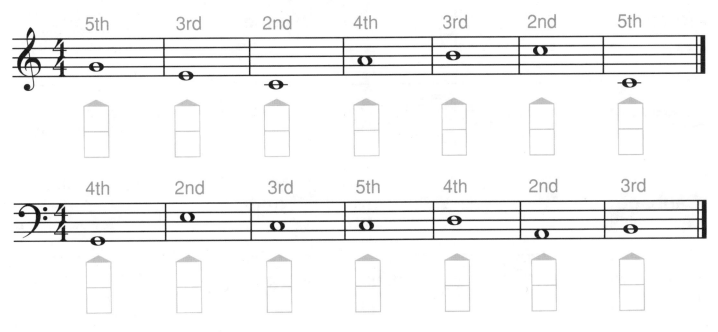

Note Review

Use with pages 62–63.

Draw lines connecting the dots on the matching boxes.

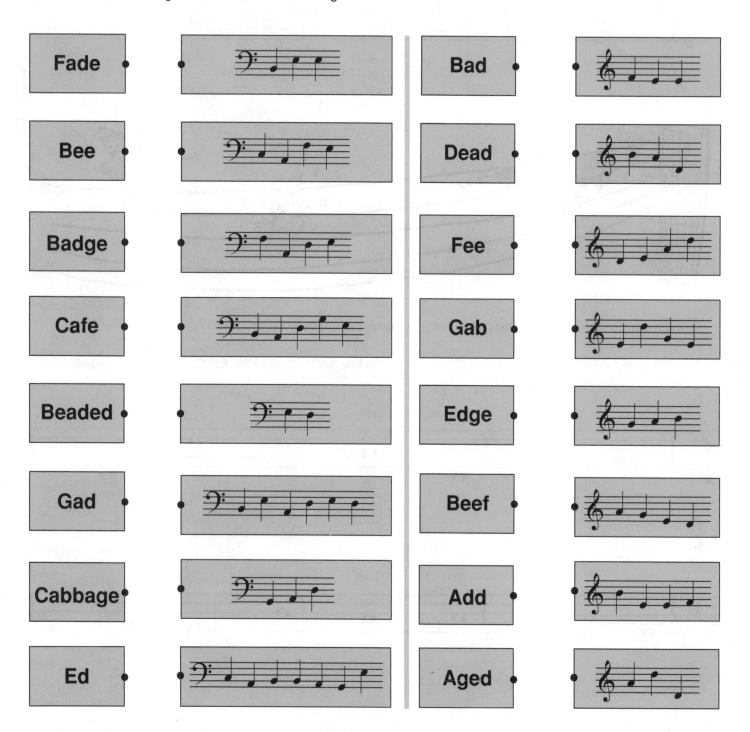

Fade

Bee

Badge

Cafe

Beaded

Gad

Cabbage

Ed

Bad

Dead

Fee

Gab

Edge

Beef

Add

Aged